BLAIRSVILLE SENIOR HIGH SCHOOL
BLAIRSVILLE, PENNA.

T 31187

L

# 18-Wheelers

by Linda Lee Maifair

Capstone Press

P.O. Box 669, Mankato, MN, U.S.A. 56002-0669

# C A P S T O N E  P R E S S

818 North Willow Street • Mankato, Minnesota 56001

Copyright © 1991 Capstone Press. All rights reserved. No part of this book may be reproduced without written permission from the publisher.

Printed in the United States of America.

*Library of Congress Cataloging-in-Publication Data*
Maifair, Linda Lee.
  18-wheelers / by Linda Lee Maifair.
  p. cm. -- (Cruisin')
  Summary: Discusses eighteen-wheelers, the different types, the work they do, and the people who drive them.
  ISBN 1-56065-073-7
  1. Tractor trailer combinations--Juvenile literature. [1. Tractor trailers. 2. Trucks.] I. Title. II. Title: Eighteen-wheelers. III. Series.
TL230.15.M35 1989
629.224--dc20

                                        89-25237
                                           CIP
                                            AC

Photo credits
Mack Trucks: 3, 6, 8, 10, 14, 19, 22, 30, 34, 36, 39
Roadway: 4, 5, 14, 16, 25, 48

# Contents

# The First Trucks

The first truck was an engine hooked to a wagon. It was built almost 100 years ago. Trucks were not very popular. They frightened delivery horses. People called trucks the "devil's wagon." Trucks were outlawed in many towns.

On July 3, 1911, a heat wave hit New York City. 1700 horses died in one day. Trucks were called in to take their place. It was a sad day for the owners of the delivery wagons. It was a lucky day for America's new trucking industry.

The emergency in New York City proved how valuable trucks could be. People found out trucks could pull harder than horses. They could carry heavier loads. They could work faster and longer. They did not need tracks, waterways, or landing fields either. Trucks were here to stay.

Today almost everything we use is delivered by truck. Trucks carry all kinds of goods. They work in all kinds of weather. They run 24 hours a day, 365 days a year. The biggest and most powerful trucks are the 18-wheelers.

This book is about 18-wheelers. You will learn about different kinds of tractor-trailers. You will read about the work they do and the people who drive them.

# What is an 18-Wheeler?

An **18-wheeler** is a truck with 18 wheels. 18-wheelers have other names, too. They are known as **tractor-trailers** or **combination-trucks** because they are a tractor and trailer combined. 10 wheels are on the tractor. 8 wheels are on the trailer.

18-wheelers are big. They can haul as much as 20 pick-up trucks. Fully loaded, they can weigh up to 80,000 pounds. That is as heavy as 30 cars. Some combinations are 65 feet long. That is the same as 5 or 6 cars parked end to end. Imagine sitting on a chair on the roof of your car. That is how high you would be if you were driving an 18-wheeler!

A **rig** is a truck with a CB radio. Because of their size, 18-wheelers are sometimes called **big rigs.**

## Tractors

The **tractor** is the front part of an 18-wheeler. Like a farm tractor, the tractor of an 18-wheeler is a powerful piece of machinery. It is used to pull all sorts of heavy equipment. It does all kinds of work.

The tractor's heavy steel **frame** supports the wheels and the chassis. The **chassis** contains the motor and the cab. The frame, chassis, wheels, motor and cab are all part of the tractor.

## Motors

It takes a lot of power to pull 40 tons of freight. An 18-wheeler's motor has as much as 475 **horsepower**. That is 2 or 3 times more pulling power than the motor in your family car.

This power comes from a **diesel engine**, named after it's inventor Rudolph Diesel. Like the motor in your car, a diesel engine is an **internal combustion engine**. The fuel burns inside the cylinder.

Gasoline engines need spark plugs to ignite the fuel. A diesel engine does not. Fuel is squirted directly into the diesel engine. The pressure of the moving pistons is so great, and the air inside the cylinder gets so hot, the fuel ignites without a spark.

The fuel burns. The pistons move up and down. The crankshaft turns the axles. The axles turn the wheels. The tractor moves.

Your car probably runs on gasoline. Diesel engines run on **diesel fuel**. Diesel fuel is an oil. It is not as refined or purified as gasoline. It is also not as expensive.

This is important to a trucker. It takes as much as 300 gallons to fill the big aluminum "saddle tanks" on each side of his tractor. His tractor-trailer uses a lot more fuel than an automobile. An 18-wheeler gets only 5 or 6 miles to the gallon. A car can travel about 4 times as far on a gallon of fuel.

Most car engines have 4 to 6 cylinders. 18-wheelers have 6 to 8. Cars with automatic transmissions usually have 4 speeds or gears. The driver of an 18-wheeler may have to go through 13 gears to get his truck rolling down the highway.

Diesel engines are tough. A car engine begins to wear out before it travels 100,000 miles. Most truckers drive that much in a year. Their diesels are built to run more than a million miles. If there were a highway between here and the moon, a trucker could make the trip in his 18-wheeler twice.

## Cabs

The **cab** of a truck is where the driver sits. Until the 1920s there were no cabs. The driver sat in an open box. His seat was a board behind the engine. He had no protection from the weather. There were no windows or windshield. If a driver had to stay out over night, he slept under the truck or in with the freight. If he was hauling cows...or pigs...he probably slept on the ground.

The cab of today's 18-wheeler looks like the cockpit of an airplane. There are gauges for everything from fuel level to air pressure. The seats are padded for comfort and built to support the driver's back on long-distance runs.

A long distance trucker may spend 6 or 8 weeks on the road. Today's truckers sleep in their trucks, not under them. They have a bed in the **sleeper box** behind the cab. Some drivers have their own TV, VCR, sink and toilet, too. The cabs and sleepers are heated in the winter and air conditioned in the summer.

Depending on where the cab and motor sit on the body of the tractor, 18-wheelers are either **cab-overs** or **conventional trucks.**

## Conventional Truck

In a **conventional truck** the motor is in front of the cab. Because the hood over the motor sticks out from the cab, they are sometimes called **long nose** trucks.

It is convenient to work on the engine of a long-nose tractor. The cab does not get in the way. The

driver does not sit right on top of the engine. This gives him a smoother ride. A long-nose truck also gives a driver more protection in a head-on collision. He has the heavy engine of his tractor between him and the other vehicle in the accident.

## Cab-Over-Engine Truck

**Cab-over-engine trucks**, or **C.O.E.'s**, have the cab built right over the engine. They are easy to recognize. The tractor is flat in the front. The hood does not stick out like it does in a conventional truck. The whole front of the cab from roof to bumper can be tilted forward, away from the motor. This makes it possible for the **mechanics** to do repairs on the engine.

Cab-overs have a shorter **wheel base** than conventional tractors. There is a shorter space between the two wheels at the front and the two sets of **dual** or double wheels at the back. C.O.E.'s need less room for turning. This makes them easier to steer in tight places. Because they are shorter, they can haul longer trailers and bigger loads. The bigger the **payload**, the more money a truck makes.

Cab-overs can have a sleeper bunk right in the cab. The first bunks were less than two feet across and so low a driver could not sit up with-

out banging his head. Modern bunks are 30 to 36 inches wide. The driver gets into the bunk by crawling behind the driving seat.

## Fifth Wheels

The **fifth-wheel** on an 18-wheeler is not really a wheel at all. It is a large, round, steel plate mounted on the back of the tractor. A **kingpin** on the trailer locks into a slot in the fifth wheel. The kingpin holds the tractor and trailer together.

Though truckers like to keep their tractors clean and polished, they make sure the fifth wheel is covered with heavy grease. The grease helps the kingpin swivel smoothly in the fifth wheel. Watch an 18-wheeler making a turn and you will see how it bends where the tractor and trailer come together. Without a fifth wheel, the tractor-trailer would not be able to bend.

## Trailers

The **trailer** or body of the truck is the part that hauls the load. It trails behind the tractor.

A **semi-trailer** only has wheels at the rear. Sometimes people call 18-wheelers **semis.** Semi-trailers need a tractor to hold up their front end. When the trailer is parked in a lot the front rests on **dollies**.

Dollies are legs with wheels at the end. Sometimes the dollies have flat plates called **sandshoes** instead of wheels. Sandshoes help protect the pavement when a heavy trailer has to sit in one place. Dollies are raised up out of the way when the trailer is hooked to a tractor.

The size and shape of the trailer depend on the kind of freight it carries. Since every fifth wheel is exactly the same, a company can use one tractor to pull many different kinds of trailers. One at a time, of course.

## Kinds of Trailers

A **van** is like a big metal box on wheels. It carries dry goods. For example, a moving van is a trailer used to haul furniture.

A **reefer** is a refrigerated van. The ceiling, walls and floor are insulated to keep the freight hot or cold. Reefers have their own cooling units. They haul food which would spoil in a regular truck.

A **livestock** van has slats so the animals can get the air they need. Some livestock vans have decks. They carry small animals like chickens or sheep on the bottom. Larger animals like cattle ride on the top. Truckers have nicknames for these trailers. Can you guess what kind of livestock travels in a "cackle crate"?

**19**

A **flatbed** is like a floor on wheels. It has no sides. It can haul loads wider than itself. You have probably seen heavy road equipment riding on the back of a flatbed trailer. A big bulldozer would never fit in a van!

**Tankers** carry liquids. Some tankers carry chemicals and fuel oil. Tankers that carry liquid food are lined with glass or stainless steel. That makes them easier to keep clean. Tankers are dangerous to drive. When the truck stops, the liquid inside the tank keeps moving. This can push the truck into another vehicle.

A trailer with wheels at both ends is called a **full trailer**. In some states, on big highways, truckers are allowed to pull two trailers. A semi-trailer is hooked to the fifth wheel. A full trailer is pulled behind the semi. These double trailers are known as **tandems** or **double bottoms**.

# Driving an 18-Wheeler

Driving an 18-wheeler is a lot different than driving a car. The 18-wheeler is longer, wider, higher and heavier. It has more gauges and gears.

An 18-wheeler "bends in the middle." On an icy road, the tractor-trailer may **jackknife**. The trailer turns on the fifth wheel and begins to travel faster than the tractor! It takes a good driver to keep the trailer from coming all the way around and crashing into his cab.

## Truck Driving Schools

Some men and women go to special schools to learn how to drive an 18-wheeler. The Professional Drivers Academy in Milton, Pennsylvania, is an example. Their course takes 12 weeks. It costs about $3000. Students do not hop up behind the wheel and pull out on a highway. They spend 3 weeks in the classroom and on the practice lot first.

What would you study at a truck driving school? All the things the driver of an 18-wheeler needs to know to operate his vehicle safely and legally.

Truckers are supposed to inspect their trucks before they take them on the road each day. They must be sure the lights, brakes, turn signals and tires are in working order. This is called a **pre-trip circle check**. The driver makes a circle of the truck as he checks it over. Student drivers study equipment inspection.

Weight limits and hauling restrictions are different from state to state. Cross-country drivers must obey the laws in each state. Student drivers

study trucking laws and regulations.

Big rig truckers are not supposed to drive more than 60 hours a week. They cannot drive more than 10 hours without an 8 hour rest period. Professional drivers keep a daily log of their driving and resting time, even when they are on vacation. Student drivers learn how to fill out these logs.

A truck may break down on the road. Drivers can save time and money by making small repairs themselves. They can prevent some of these breakdowns with good **maintenance** or care of their motors. Students study engines and trans-missions.

Some drivers have to load the freight they carry. Loads must be tied down. A shifting or unbalanced load can cause a trailer to turn over. Loose loads must be covered. Blowing gravel could chip the windshield of a car following the tractor-trailer. Loose sand on the highway could make it slippery. Student drivers must know how to load their 18-wheelers.

A tractor and trailer must be **coupled** or hooked together properly. If a tractor pulls away without its trailer, the lines that connect the trailer's lights and air brakes can be torn loose. A trailer that comes loose on a highway could cause a fatal accident. Student drivers practice coupling and uncoupling the tractors and trailers.

Finally a student driver gets to take a rig out on the highway! He spends 9 weeks on the road, making real deliveries. He does not go alone. His 18-wheeler becomes a school on wheels. His driving partner is his teacher! A student does not get to **solo**, or drive by himself, until he has had nearly 500 hours of study and practice driving.

## Getting A License

To get a license to drive a tractor-trailer **interstate**, from one state to another, you must be at least 21. You have to fill out logs and understand regulations and road signs. You have to pass both a written exam and a road test.

To pass the road test, a driver must do a pre-trip circle check. He must prove he can park parallel to the curb and back up his rig safely. He must obey road signs and signals. He has to stop and start on a hill and make left and right turns. A driver must couple and uncouple the tractor and trailer correctly. He must also **dock** the vehicle as if he were backing into the loading dock of a factory.

These things are harder to do in an 18-wheeler than they would be in a car. It is hard to park close to the curb without running over it when you have 48 feet of trailer behind you. It is more

complicated to start on a hill when you have 13 gears to worry about. It is difficult to make left hand turns without running over street signs or telephone poles. To back up a car, the driver turns the steering wheel in the same direction he wants the rear of the car to go. The driver of an 18-wheeler has to turn the wheel in the opposite direction.

Drivers of 18-wheelers work long hours. Their job has a lot of worry or stress. They must be in good physical condition to get a license. They have to pass a complete physical exam and drug screen every 2 years to keep it.

## Keeping Your License

A new federal law makes it illegal for a driver to have more than one 18-wheeler license. In the past, a driver who lost his license in one state could still drive. All he needed was a spare license from somewhere else. Now a driver will have only one license. If he loses that, he will not be able to drive at all.

How does a driver lose his license? Driving while drunk or drugged. Leaving the scene of an accident. Using a truck to commit a crime like hauling illegal drugs or stolen goods. Driving recklessly or getting too many speeding tickets.

A police officer can put an "out of service" sticker on any tractor-trailer he thinks is unsafe. The vehicle cannot be driven on the highways until it is fixed. A driver can be declared "out of service" too if his log shows he has driven more hours than he should. He will be taken off the road if he is caught hauling a rig that is over the weight limit. He may have to pay thousands of dollars in fines for such violations.

## Women Drivers

In the early days of trucking, tractor-trailers were difficult to steer. Life on the road was hard. Few women knew how to drive 18-wheelers. Most companies would not hire them.

Roads and driving conditions have improved. So have trucks. Power steering makes them easier to drive. Special equipment is used to unload heavy freight. Strength is no longer a requirement for the driver of an 18-wheeler. Women have proven themselves to be skillful drivers.

There are nearly 2 million people qualified to drive tractor-trailers. About 80,000 of these drivers are women. Just like male drivers, some of these women drive their own 18-wheelers. Some work for big trucking companies. Some "team" with another driver.

# Working For A Trucking Company

In World War I trucks were used to carry troops and supplies. The army bought more than 250,000 trucks in one year. After the war, the army put the trucks up for sale. Some people bought a **fleet** of several trucks. They started the earliest trucking companies. Their companies were the first **common carriers.**

Common carriers carry goods for anybody who wants to hire their trucks and drivers. People pay them to haul all sorts of freight. The heavier the goods and the farther the delivery, the more money the trucking company makes.

Most large trucking companies have their own requirements for drivers of 18-wheelers. A license is not enough. For example, at Roadway Express a driver has to be at least 23 years old. He has to have a good driving record. He must pass a physical exam and drug test. He has to have at least one full year of driving experience. Some companies require two or three years.

How does a new driver get experience? Working for a small trucking company. Working for a business that uses 18-wheelers to deliver its product. Taking a job on the loading dock or "jockeying" rigs around the company yard.

Graduating from a good driving school usually helps a driver get a job. Some companies even have schools and training programs of their own.

## Advantages of Driving for a Company

Most drivers of 18-wheelers work for one particular company. Some deliver the same thing – like potato chips or TV sets – all the time. They drive for the company that produces these items. Others haul all kinds of freight. They work for a common carrier. Either way, there are good reasons to work for a company.

Company drivers do not have to pay for the trucks they drive. Companies have their own mechanics. They keep the trucks in safe working order. If a truck breaks down on the road, the company pays to have it fixed.

A company driver does not have to look for work to do. Company sales people find new loads for the truck to carry. The **dispatcher** at the **terminal** or truck garage will tell the driver where to pick up and deliver a load. If a driver has to wait for a truck to be unloaded, or drive 500 hundred miles to pick up a new load, the company will pay him for his time.

Many company drivers work in teams. One drives while the other sleeps. The truck can keep moving. Teams can cover more miles in less time than a solo driver who has to pull off the road to rest. A team can drive from New York to California in less than three days. Some teams are husbands and wives who enjoy traveling and working together.

# Owning an 18-Wheeler

**Independent drivers** work for themselves. They are called **owner-operators**. They own their own trucks and operate their own businesses. They do not work for a trucking company. There are more than 100,000 owner-operators.

Most independent drivers start with a trucking company. They save the money to buy their own tractor. Some independent truckers own their own trailers, too. Others use trailers supplied by the people who hire them.

A company gives the independent trucker a load to deliver. It is up to him to get it there safely and on time. What route and schedules he follows is up to him. Most independent truckers like the responsibility. They like being their own boss.

But owning an 18-wheeler is expensive. Seventy percent of what an independent driver earns is spent on his business. That means every time he earns a dollar, seventy cents goes to pay for his truck. Thirty cents is left for the trucker.

A new truck will cost more than $100,000. That is as much as eight new cars. A trucker only has four or five years to pay for his truck. Payments can run from $1500 to $2000 a month.

The independent trucker has a lot of other bills to pay. Every time he fills his fuel tanks it costs him $300 to $500. Both the state and federal government collect fuel taxes to pay for highway construction and repair. A truck is much heavier than a car. It puts a bigger strain on the roadways. 18-wheelers pay extra road use taxes. These taxes can add up to more than $6000 a year. A trucking company pays these taxes on their vehicles. An independent trucker has to pay them himself.

Insurance on a tractor can cost $350 a month. That is 4 or 5 times what it would cost on a new car. Turnpike and bridge tolls are higher for truckers too. Truckers can pay as much as $150 a day in tolls. A car may pay fifty cents to a dollar to cross a toll bridge. The trucker pays $4 to $21 dollars to go over the same bridge in his 18-wheeler. A company driver gets reimbursed, or paid back, by his company. An independent driver does not.

If his truck breaks down on the road, an independent driver has to pay to fix it. Even a small repair can cost him a lot of money. His truck cannot be on the road, making money, while it is in the repair shop. A missed delivery can cost a trucker several thousand dollars.

A company driver gets paid for **down time** when the truck is being loaded and unloaded. An independent driver only gets paid for the time his 18 wheels are moving and hauling freight. Sometimes a trucker has to drive his tractor hundreds of miles to pick up a new load. A company driver would be paid for that time. An independent driver is not paid for the mileage. In fact, he has to pay for the fuel to get there.

## Buying an 18-Wheeler

When you want to buy an 18-wheeler you go to a truck dealer. He will have several different models and styles on display. He may even have used trucks for sale. Like used cars, these vehicles are cheaper to buy.

The driver tells the truck dealer exactly what he wants. The dealer orders the truck from the company. There are several companies to choose from. Peterbilt, Freightliner, Kenworth, Cumings, Caterpillar, GMC, White, Ford and International are a few.

Some companies, like Mack Truck, have been in business a long time. Mack started in 1900, more than 90 years ago. Since then they have manufactured more than a million Mack trucks. They have their own mascot, the Mack bulldog. He sits on the hood of every Mack truck.

At Mack, the cab and chassis are assembled in one factory. The motors and transmissions are made in another. It takes about 2 days to put a tractor together on the Mack assembly line. An automobile factory can produce 300 cars a day. Mack produces about 40 trucks a day. Sometimes they make one truck for one driver. Sometimes they make a whole fleet of matching trucks for a company.

Drivers are anxious to get their new trucks. They want to be the first to drive them. Often a trucker will go to the factory to pick up his new truck and drive it home.

# Champions on 18 Wheels

In the movies, truckers are rough and tough. They wear "western" clothes, hats, and boots. Some drivers fit this picture. Some do not. Some

truckers do not like the "cowboy" image. Some do. Some drivers refer to regional and national truck-driving championships as "rodeos." Others just call them "competitions."

Whatever you call them, it takes a special driver to win a championship on 18 wheels. A driver cannot enter an American Trucking Association competition if he has been in an accident in the year before the contest.

The contestants do more than drive. They are judged on appearance, knowledge of safe driving rules and understanding of the trucking industry. They are even tested on special skills like fire-fighting and first-aid.

The driving competition is called a **field-test**. One part of the field test is a pre-trip inspection. All the contestants inspect the same vehicle. The vehicle has several things wrong with it. The driver who finds the most violations and safety problems gets the most points.

The driving test includes things like coupling, backing, and parking. It also includes special problems or obstacles. A driver may have to weave in and out around a line of highway markers. This is very hard to do with a full-length trailer. He may have to back down a zig-zag course between narrowly spaced fences. He has to do it without backing into anything. Once he starts the course, he cannot stop his truck. He cannot pull forward and back up again. He has to run through the obstacles in one smooth motion.

It is a big honor and achievement to win a truck-driving competition. Sometimes the winning driver gets a special belt buckle to wear.

## Knights of the Road

Whether they compete in rodeos or not, most truckers are good drivers. They have to be. Their living depends on their driving record.

The truck driver's safety record is nearly twice as good as the car driver's. In 6 out of 10 car-truck accidents, the driver of the automobile is at fault. 18-wheelers are involved in less than 2 1/2% of all accidents.

Good truck drivers are courteous on the high-way. They will blink their lights to let you know when it is safe to pull back in front of them after passing. They will pull over, if they can, to let faster traffic pass. Truckers often stop to help stranded motorists. Some people call them the "knights of the road."

Automobile drivers need to be courteous in return. Professional truck drivers think young car drivers should learn more about trucks in their driver's education classes. Here are some things they think automobile drivers should know:

An 18-wheeler cannot pull onto a highway as quickly as a car. The driver has 13 gears to get through. His vehicle is heavier. It takes him longer to build up speed.

An 80,000 pound, fully-loaded tractor-trailer cannot move uphill as fast as a 2,500 pound car. The driver is not holding up traffic on purpose. He wants to get his load delivered as quickly as he can. That is how he earns his money.

The trucker has 40 tons of freight holding him back when he is going uphill. He also has 40 tons of freight pushing him forward when he goes down the other side. An impatient car driver who cuts in front of a truck may get run over.

A car driver going 55 miles an hour needs 6 car lengths to stop his car. An 18-wheeler is as long as 5 or 6 cars. The driver needs the length of 30 cars to get his vehicle stopped.

Most car-truck accidents happen at intersections. An 18-wheeler must pull into the left lane to make a right hand turn. That is the only way the driver can get the back of his trailer around the corner without wiping out a telephone pole or running up over the sidewalk. Car drivers who are not paying attention do not see the truck's right-turn signal. They pull into the right lane to get by the truck. The driver of the truck cannot see the other vehicle. He makes the turn and hits the car.

Truckers need to be alert and careful. They need to use good common sense when they drive. Automobile drivers who share the road with them need to do the same.

# Talkin' Truckin'

"The jockey of the bull rack was on the peg, doing double nickels, when he had bubble trouble and his donut went flat on the big slab."

A new language? No, just truck talk. Can you figure it out? It means a professional driver in a cattle truck was driving the speed limit, going 55 miles an hour, when he had tire trouble…a flat tire on the highway.

All big rigs have a **CB** or **Citizen's Band** radio. Truckers use the CB's for emergency calls and directions. They also use them to talk to their **good buddies**, the other drivers on the road. When they **have their ears on**, or are using their

CB's truckers have a language of their own.

Here are some expressions you might use if you were talkin' truckin' in an 18-wheeler:

A **4-wheeler** is an automobile. A **winkin' blinkin'** is a school bus. A **cackle crate** is a chicken truck.

A state policeman is a **Bear**, sometimes called **Smokey**. **Bear trap** is another name for a radar check. A **bear bite** is a speeding ticket. **Feeding the bears** means paying a traffic fine. Smokeys ride in **bubble tops** or police cruisers with lights on the roof. A **Smokey with ears** is a policeman with a CB radio.

A weigh station where police check to be sure a truck is not carrying too much freight is called a **chicken coop**. A toll booth is a **piggy bank**. **Lettuce** is the money you'd use to pay the toll.

Someone who drives a truck for a living is a **gearjammer**. A speeding driver is an **aviator**. An aviator probably has the **hammer down**. The **hammer** is the accelerator pedal. A **superskate** is a very fast car.

A rough riding truck is a **kidney buster.** A vehicle that is out of gas or diesel is **running on sailboat fuel** (air). A bad driver is a **yo-yo**. The **front door** is the first truck in a **convoy** or line of trucks traveling together. The last truck is the **back door.**

With a little practice you and your friends can talk truckin' too. Be sure you pay attention. You do not want somebody calling you an **alligator** (all mouth and no ears) or saying you have **peanut butter ears!**

## Finding Out More:

If you want to know more about 18-wheelers, the library is a good place to start. Look in the card catalog for books on transportation, engines, trucks, trucking, tractor-trailers, and big rigs.

You might go to a truck stop to see how many different kinds of tractors and trailers you can find. You could visit a truck dealer or truck garage. You could even invite a trucker to come to your school. Who knows, he or she might drive up on 18 wheels and let you see inside a big rig!

# Glossary

**Baffles:** Partitions in a tanker to divide the load and slow down the movement of liquid freight.

**Cab:** Where the driver sits in the tractor.

**Cab-over truck:** A truck with the cab built over the top of the engine. Also called cab-over-engine or C.O.E.

**Chassis:** The part of the tractor that contains the motor and cab. The chassis sits on the frame.

**Combination truck:** An 18-wheeler. A truck made up of a tractor and trailer combined.

**Conventional truck:** A long-nose truck which has the engine built in front of the cab instead of on top.

**Common carrier:** A trucking company that hauls freight for anybody who hires its trucks and drivers.

**Couple:** To back up the tractor to the trailer, hooking the fifth wheel and kingpin together.

**Diesel engine:** An engine that runs on diesel fuel instead of gasoline.

**Dispatcher:** The person at the trucking terminal who lets the drivers know where and when to pick up and deliver a load.

**Dock:** To back a truck up to a loading area. The loading area is also called the dock.

**Dollies:** Legs with wheels or sandshoes used to hold up the front of a semi-trailer when it is not hooked to a tractor.

**Double bottoms:** Two trailers pulled by the same tractor. One is a semi-trailer hooked to the tractor. The other is a full trailer pulled behind the semi.

**Dual tires:** Two tires running together at the end of an axle. An 18-wheeler has 8 sets of dual wheels.

**18-wheeler:** A tractor-trailer with 10 wheels on the tractor and 8 wheels on the trailer.

**Field test:** The driving part of a "rodeo" or truck driving competition.

**Fifth wheel:** A round, flat metal plate on the back of a tractor. The kingpin fits into a slot on the fifth wheel and holds the tractor-trailer together.

**Flatbed:** A trailer with no sides.

**Fleet:** A number of trucks owned by the same company.

**Frame:** The steel framework that support a tractor's wheels and chassis.

**Full trailer:** A trailer with wheels at both the front and back.

**Horsepower:** The pulling power of an engine.

**Independent trucker:** A driver who works for himself instead of a company.

**Internal combustion engine:** An engine that burns its fuel inside the cylinder.

**Interstate:** From one state to another.

**Jackknife:** A dangerous situation where the trailer of an 18-wheeler slides around toward the cab.

**Lease:** To rent the use of a truck. Independent truckers often lease their trucks to trucking companies.

**Long nose:** A conventional truck where the motor sits in front of the cab.

**Mechanic:** A person who works on and fixes engines.

**Moving violation:** A traffic ticket for something a driver does while his truck is moving. Speeding is an example.

**Owner-operator:** An independent trucker who owns his own truck and operates his own business.

**Payload:** The freight a tractor-trailer is hauling. The driver gets paid for delivering the load.

**Pre-trip circle check:** An inspection a trucker must make before he takes his rig on the road.

**Reefer:** A refrigerated van. Insulated to keep freight hot or cold.

**Rig:** A truck with a CB radio. 18-wheelers are called big rigs.

**Sandshoes:** Flat plates at the bottom of dollies. Used to protect the pavement when a heavy trailer has to sit in one place.

**Semi-trailer:** A trailer with wheels only at the back. 18-wheelers are sometimes called semis.

**Sleeper box:** A separate sleeping area that sits on a tractor frame behind the cab.

**Tandem:** Two trailers being pulled by the same

tractor. Also the two sets of wheels on the back of the trailer.

**Tanker:** A trailer used to haul liquids.

**Terminal:** Where a trucking company keeps its trucks.

**Tractor:** The front part of an 18-wheeler. The part with the motor.

**Tractor-trailer:** An 18-wheeler. A combination truck that has a tractor in front and a trailer in the back.

**Trailer:** The part of a tractor-trailer that holds the freight. Sometimes called the body of the truck.

**Van:** A type of trailer. A big metal box on wheels. Used for dry goods.

**Wheel base:** The distance between the front wheels and the back wheels.